Secret of the

This ancient esoteric treatise was transmitted orally for centuries before being recorded on a series of wooden tablets in the eighth century. It was recorded by a member of the Religion of Light, whose leader was the Taoist adept Lu Yen (also known as Lu Yen and Lu "Guest of the Cavern"). It is said that Lu Tzu became one of the Eight Immortals using these methods. The ideas have been traced back to Persia and the Zarathustra tradition and its roots in the Egyptian Hermetic tradition.

This book has been published by:

Contact: sales@nuvisionpublications.com

URL: http://www.nuvisionpublications.com

Publishing Date: 2007

ISBN# 1-59547-919-8

Please see my website for several books created for
education, research and entertainment.

Specializing in rare, out-of-print books still in demand.

Contents

HEAVENLY CONSCIOUSNESS OF THE HEART

Master Lu Tzu said: That which exists through itself is called Meaning. (Tao). Meaning has neither name nor force. It is the one essence, the one primordial spirit. Essence and life cannot be seen. It is contained in the Light of Heaven. The light of Heaven cannot be seen. It is contained in the two eyes. Today I will be your guide and will first reveal to you the secret of the Golden Flower of the Great One, and, starting from that, I will explain the rest in detail. *because it's contained in the eyes it cannot be seen by the eyes*

The Great One is the term given to that which has nothing above it. The secret of the magic of life consists in using action in order to achieve non-action. One must not wish to leave out the steps between and penetrate directly. The maxim handed down to us is to take in hand the work on the essence. In doing this it is important not to follow the wrong road. *General Truth* *GOD* *other religions? other deity?*

non-action

The Golden Flower is the Light. What color has the light? One uses the Golden Flower as an image. It is the true power of the transcendent Great One. The phrase, "The lead of the water-region has but one taste," refers to it. The work on the circulation of the Light depends entirely on the backward-flowing movement, so that the thoughts are gathered together (the place of Heavenly Consciousness, the Heavenly Heart). The Heavenly Heart lies between sun and moon (i.e., the two eyes).

it has to be experienced first - to truly gather it all together

the mind *when space is irrelevant?*

The Book of the Yellow Castle says: In the field of the square inch of the house of the square foot, life can be regulated. The house of the square foot is the face. The field of the square inch in the face: What could that be other than the Heavenly Heart? In the middle of the square inch dwells the splendor. In the purple hall of the city of jade dwells the god of utmost emptiness and life. The Confucians call it the center of emptiness; the Buddhists, the terrace of life; the Taoists, the ancestral land, or

wrinkle in brain?

the body is just that, a body, until light guides it to enlightenment.

the yellow castle, or the dark pass, or the space of former Heaven. The Heavenly Heart is like the dwelling place, the Light is the master. Therefore when the Light circulates, the powers of the whole body arrange themselves before its throne, just as when a holy king has taken possession of the capital and has laid down the fundamental rules of order, all the states approach with tribute, or, just as when the master is quiet and calm, menservants and maids obey his orders of their own accord, and each does his work.

*Therefore you only have to make the Light circulate: that is the deepest and most wonderful secret*The Light is easy to move, but difficult to fix. If it is allowed to go long enough in a circle, then it crystallizes itself: that is the natural spirit -body. This crystallized spirit is formed beyond the nine Heavens. It is the condition of which it is said in the Book of the Seal of the Heart: Silently in the morning thou fliest upward.

In carrying out this fundamental truth you need to seek for no other methods, but must only concentrate your thoughts on it. The book Leng Yen says: By collecting the thoughts one can fly and will be born in Heaven. Heaven is not the wide blue sky, but the place where the body is made in the house of the creative. If one keeps this up for a long time, there develops quite naturally in addition to the body, yet another spirit-body.

The Golden Flower is the Elixir of Life (literally, golden ball, golden pill). Here is a secret charm, which, although it works very accurately, is yet so fluent that it needs extreme intelligence and clarity, and complete absorption and calm. People without this highest degree of intelligence and understanding do not find the way to apply the charm; People without this utmost capacity for concentration and calm cannot keep fast hold of it.

indigo & crystal children.

THE PRIMORDIAL SPIRIT AND THE CONSCIOUS SPIRIT

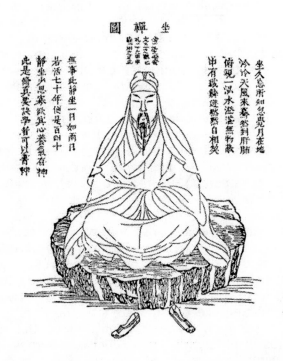

We are miniscule compared to the Light.

Master Lu Tzu said: In comparison with Heaven and earth, man is like a mayfly. But compared to the Great Meaning, Heaven and earth, too, are like a bubble and a shadow. Only the primordial spirit and the true essence overcome time and space.

The power of the seed, like Heaven and earth, is subject to mortality, but the primordial spirit is beyond the polar differences. Here is the place whence Heaven and Earth derive their being. When students understand how to grasp the primordial spirit, they overcome the polar opposites of Light and darkness and tarry no longer in the three worlds. But only he who has looked on essence in its (original manifestation) is able to do this. *experience first-understanding second*

~~become the~~ born devine !

When men are set free from the womb the primordial spirit dwells in the square inch (between the eyes), but the conscious spirit dwells below in the heart. This lower fleshly heart has the shape of a large peach: it is covered by the wings of the lungs, supported by the liver, and served by the bowels. This heart is dependent on the outside world. If a man does not eat for one day even, it feels extremely uncomfortable. If it hears something terrifying it throbs; if it hears something enraging it stops; if its is faced with death it becomes sad; if it sees something beautiful it is dazzled. But the Heavenly Heart in the head, when would it have been in the leased moved? Dost thou ask: Can the Heavenly Heart not be moved? Then I answer: How could the true thought in the square inch be moved? If it really moves, it is not well. For when ordinary men die, then it moves, but that is not good. It is best indeed if the Light has already fortified itself in a spirit body and its life force gradually penetrated the instincts and movements. But that is a secret which has not been revealed for thousands of years.

The lower heart moves like a strong, powerful commander who despises the Heavenly ruler because of his weakness, and has seized for himself the leadership of the affairs of state. But when the primordial castle can be fortified and defended, then it is as if a strong and wise ruler sat upon the throne. The two eyes start the Light circulating like two ministers at the right and left who support the ruler with all their might. When the ruler in the center is thus in order, all those rebellious heroes will present themselves with lances reversed ready to take orders.

The way to the Elixir of life recognizes as supreme magic, seed-water, spirit-fire, and thought-earth; these three. What is seed-water? It is the true, one power (eros) of former Heaven. Spirit-fire is the Light (logos). Thought-earth is the Heavenly Heart of the middle house (intuition). Spirit-fire is used for effecting, thought-earth for substance, and seed-water for the foundation. Ordinary men make their bodies through thoughts.

The body is not only the 7 ft. tall outer body. In the body is the anima. The anima, having produced consciousness, adheres to it. Consciousness depends for its origin on the anima. The anima is feminine, the substance of consciousness. As long as this consciousness is not interrupted, it continues to beget from generation to generation, and the changes of form of the anima and the transformations of substance are unceasing.

But, besides this, there is the animus in which the spirit shelters. The animus lives in the daytime in the eyes; at night it houses in the liver. When living in the eyes, it sees; when housing itself in the liver, it dreams. Dreams are the wanderings of the spirit through all nine Heavens and all the nine earths. But whoever is dull and moody on waking, and chained to his bodily form, is fettered by the anima. Therefore the concentration of the animus is effected by the circulation of the Light, and in this way the spirit is protected, the anima subjected, and consciousness is annulled. The method used by the ancients for escaping from the world consisted in burning out completely the slag of darkness in order to return to the purely creative. This is nothing more than a reduction of the anima and a bringing to perfection of the animus. And the circulation of the Light is the magical means of limiting the dark powers and gaining mastery of the anima. Even if the work is not directed toward bringing back the creative, but confines itself to the magical means of the circulation, one returns to the creative, If this method is followed, plenty of seed-water will be present of itself; the spirit-fire will be ignited, and the thought-earth will solidify and crystallize. And thus can the holy fruit mature. The scarab rolls his ball and in the ball there develops life as the effect of the undivided effort of his spiritual concentration. If now and embryo can grow in manure, and shed its skin, why should not the dwelling place of our Heavenly Heart also be able to create a body if we concentrate the spirit upon it?

The one effective, true essence (logos united with life), when it descends into the house of the creative, divides into animus and anima. The animus is in the Heavenly Heart. It is of the nature of light; it is the power of lightness and purity. It is that which we have received from the great emptiness, that which has form from the very beginning. The anima partakes of the nature of darkness. It is the power of the heavy and the turbid; it is bound to the bodily, fleshly heart. The animus loves life. The anima

animus=light
anima=darkness

seeks death. All sensuous pleasures and impulses to anger are effects of the anima; it is the conscious spirit which after death is nourished on blood, but which, during life, is in direst need. Darkness returns to darkness and like things attract each other. But the pupil understands how to <u>distill the dark anima</u> so that it transforms itself into Light.

CIRCULATION OF THE LIGHT AND PROTECTION OF THE CENTER

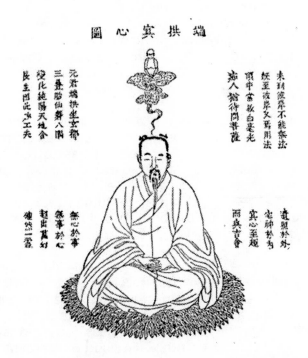

端拱冥心圖

Master Lu Tzu said: Since when has the expression "circulation of the Light" been revealed? It was revealed by the "true men of the beginning of form". When the Light is allowed to move in a circle, all the powers of Heaven and earth, of the light and the dark, are crystallized. That is what is described as seed-like, or purification of the power, or purification of the concept. When one begins to apply this magic, it is as if, in the middle of one's being, there was a non-being. When in the course of time the

Spirit-body.

work is finished, and beyond the body is another body, it is as if, in the middle of the non-being, there were a being. Only after a completed work of a hundred days will the Light be real, then only will it become spirit-fire. After a hundred days, there develops by itself in the middle of the Light, a point of the true Light-pole. Suddenly there develops a seed pearl. It is as if man and woman embraced and a conception took place. Then one must be quite still in order to await it. The circulation of the Light is the epoch of fire.

In the midst of primal becoming, the radiance of the Light is the determining thing. In the physical world it is the sun; in man the eye. The emanation and dissemination of spiritual consciousness is chiefly brought about by this power when it is directed outward (flown downward). Therefore the meaning of the Golden Flower depends wholly on the backward-flowing method. *is it diff. for everyone?*

Circulation of the Light is not only a circulation of the seed-blossom of the body, but it is, in the first place, a circulation of the true, creative, formative powers. It has to do, not with a momentary fantasy, but with the exhaustion of the circular course (soul wanderings) of all the eons. Therefore a breath-pause means a year – according to human reckoning – and a hundred years measured by the long night of the nine paths (of reincarnation).

After a person has the one tone of individualization behind them, they will be born outward according to the circumstances, and not until he is old will he turn a single time to the backward-flowing way. The force of the Light exhausts itself and trickles away. That brings the nine-fold darkness (of rebirths) into the world. In the book Leng Yen it is said: By concentrating the *wrong* thoughts, one can fly; by concentrating the desires, one falls. *path.* When a pupil takes little care of his thoughts and much care of his desires, he gets into the path of depravity. Only through contemplation and quietness does true intuition arise; for that, the backward-flowing method is necessary.

In the book of the Secret Correspondences, it is said: Release is in the eye. In the Simple Questions of the Yellow Ruler, it is said: The seed-blossom of the human body must be concentrated upward in the empty space. That refers to it. Immortality is contained in this sentence and also the overcoming of the world is contained in it. That is the common goal of all religions.

both physical and mental clarity is needed.

The Light is not in the body alone, neither is it only outside the body. Mountains and rivers and the great earth are lit by sun and moon; all that is this Light. Therefore it is not only within the body. Understanding and clarity, knowing and enlightenment, and all motion (of the spirit), are likewise this Light; therefore it is not just something outside the body. The Light-flower of Heaven and earth fills all thousand spaces. But also the Light-flower of one body passes through Heaven and covers the earth. Therefore, just as the Light is circulating, so Heaven and earth, mountains and rivers, are all rotating with it at the same time. To concentrate the seed-flower of the human body above in the eyes, that is the great key of the human body. Children, take heed! If for a day you do not practice meditation, this Light streams out, who knows whither? If you only meditate for a quarter of an hour, you can set ten thousand eons and a thousand births at rest. All methods take their source in quietness. This marvelous magic cannot be fathomed.

But when the work is started, one must press on from the obvious to the profound, from the course to the fine. Everything depends on there being no interruption. The beginning and the end of the work must be one. In between there are cooler and warmer moments, that goes without saying. But the goal must be to reach the breadth of Heaven and the depths of the sea, so that all methods seem quite easy and taken for granted. Only then do we have it in hand.

All holy men have bequeathed this to one another: nothing is possible without contemplation. When Confucious says: knowing brings one to the goal; or when Buddha calls it: the view of the Heart; or Lao Tzu says: inward vision, it is all the same.

Anyone can talk about reflection, but he cannot master it if he does not know what the word means. What has to be changed by reflection is the self-conscious heart, which has to direct itself toward that point where the formative spirit is not yet manifest. Within our 6 ft. body, we must strive for the form which existed

xix

before the laying down of Heaven and earth. If today people sit and meditate only one or two hours, looking only at their own egos, and call it contemplation, how can anything come of it?

The two founders of Buddhism and Taoism have taught that one should look at the end of one's nose. But they did not mean that one should fasten one's thoughts to the end of the nose. Neither did they mean that, while the eyes were looking at the end of the nose, the thoughts should be concentrated on the yellow middle. Wherever the eye looks, the heart is directed also. How can the glance be directed at the same time upward (yellow middle), and downward (end of the nose), or alternating, so that it is now up, now down? All that means confusing the finger with which one points to the moon with the moon itself.

What is really meant by this? The expression, "end of the nose," is very cleverly chosen. The nose must serve the eyes as a guiding line. If one is not guided by the nose, either one opens wide the eyes and looks into the distance, so that the nose is not seen, or the lids shut too much, so that the eyes close, and again the nose is not seen. But when the eyes are opened too wide, one makes the mistake of directing them outward, whereby one is easily distracted. If they are closed too much then one makes the mistake of letting them turn inward, whereby one easily sinks into a dreamy reverie. Only when the eyelids are sunk properly halfway, is the end of the nose seen in just the right way. Therefore it is taken as a guiding line. The main thing is to lower the eyelids in the right way, and then allow the Light to stream in of itself, without trying to force the Light to stream in by a concentrated effort. Looking at the nose serves only as the beginning of the inner concentration, so that the eyes are brought into the right direction for looking, and then are held to the guiding line; after that, one can let it be. That is the way a mason hangs up a plumb line. As soon as he has hung it up, he guides his work by it without continually bothering himself to look at the plumb line. Fixating contemplation is a Buddhist method which by no means has been handed down as a secret.

On looks with both eyes at the end of the nose, sits upright and in a comfortable position, and holds the heart to the center in the midst of conditions (on the fixed pole in the flight of phenomena). In Taoism it is called the yellow middle, in Buddhism the center in the midst of conditions. The two are the same. It does not necessarily mean the middle of the head. It is only a matter of fixing one's thinking on the point that lies exactly between the two eyes. Then all is well. The Light is something extremely mobile. When one fixes the thought on the midpoint between the two eyes, the Light streams in of its own accord. It is not necessary to direct the attention especially to the central castle. In these few words the most important thing is contained.

"The center in the midst of conditions," is a very fine expression. The center is omnipresent; everything is contained in it; it is connected with the release of the release of the whole process of creation. The condition is the portal. The condition, that is the fulfillment of this condition, makes the beginning, but it does not bring about the rest with inevitable necessity. The meaning of these two words is very fluid and subtle.

Fixating contemplation is indispensable, it ensures the strengthening of illumination. Only one must not stay sitting rigidly if worldly thoughts come up, but one must examine where the thought is, where it began, and where it fades out. Nothing is gained by pushing reflection further, One must be content to see where the thought arose, and not seek beyond the point of origin; for to find the heart (consciousness), to get behind consciousness with consciousness - that cannot be done. We want to bring the status of the heart together in rest – that is true contemplation. What contradicts it is false contemplation. This leads to no goal. When the flight of thoughts keeps extending farther, one should stop and begin contemplating. Let one contemplate and then start concentrating again. That is the double method of strengthening the illumination. It means the circular course of the light. The circular course is fixation. The Light is contemplation. (Fixation without contemplation is circulation without Light. Contemplation without fixation is Light without circulation.)

xxi

CIRCULATION OF THE LIGHT AND MAKING THE BREATHING RHYTHMICAL

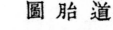

Master Lu Tzu said: The decision must be carried out with a whole heart, and, the result no sought for; the result will come of itself. In the first period of release there are chiefly two mistakes: laziness and distraction. But that can be remedied; the heart must not enter into the breathing too completely. Breathing comes from the heart. What comes out of the heart is breath. When the heart stirs, there develops breath-power. Breath-power is originally transformed activity of the heart. When our hearts go very fast they imperceptibly pass into fantasies which are always accompanied by the drawing of a breath, because this inner and outer breathing hangs together like tone and echo. Daily we draw innumerable breaths and have an equal number of fantasy-representations. And thus the clarity of the spirit is depleted just as wood dries out and ashes die.

Should a man have no images in his mind? One cannot be without images. Should one not breathe? One cannot do without breathing. The best way is to make a cure out of the illness. Since heart and breath are mutually dependent, the circulation of the Light must be united with the rhythm of breathing. For this, Light of the ear is above all necessary. There is a Light of the eye and a Light of the ear. The Light of the eye is the united Light of the sun and moon outside. The Light of the ear is the united seed of sun and moon within. The seed is also the Light in crystallized form. Both have the same origin and are different only in name. Therefore, understanding (ear) and clarity (eye) are one and the same effective Light.

In sitting down, after dropping the lids, one establishes a plumb-line with the eyes and shifts the Light downward. But if the transposition downward is not successful, then the heart is directed toward listening to the breathing. One should not be able to hear with the ear the outgoing and inhaling of the breath. What one hears is that it has no tone. As soon as it has tone, the breathing is rough and superficial, and does not penetrate into what is fine. Then the heart must be made quite light and insignificant. The more it is released, the less important it becomes; the less important, the quieter. All at once it becomes so quiet that it stops. Then the true breathing is manifested and the form of the heart can be made conscious. When the heart is light, the breathing is light, for every movement of the heart brings about breathing power. If breathing is light, the heart is light, for every movement of the breath affects the heart. In order to steady the heart, one begins by cultivating the breathing power. The heart cannot be influenced directly. Therefore the breathing power is used as a handle, and this is what is called protecting the collected breathing power.

Children, do you not understand the nature of motion? Motion can be produced by outside means. It is only another name for mastery. One can make the heart move merely by running. Should one not be able to bring it to rest then by concentrated quietness? The great holy ones who knew how the heart and breathing power mutually influence one another, have thought out an easier procedure as a way of helping posterity.

In the Book of the Elixir, it is said: The hen can hatch her eggs because her heart is always listening. That is an important magic spell. The reason the hen can hatch her eggs is because of the power to heat. But the power of the heat can only warm the shells; it cannot penetrate into the interior. Therefore with her heart she conducts this power inward. This she does with her hearing. In this way ash concentrates her whole heart. When the heart penetrates, the power penetrates, and the chick receives the power of the heart and begins to live. Therefore a hen, even when she has left her eggs, always has the attitude of listening with a bent ear. Thus the concentration of the spirit is not interrupted. Because the concentration of the spirit suffers no interruption, neither does the power of heat suffer interruption day or night, and the spirit awakes to life. The awakening of the spirit is accomplished because the heart has first died. When a man can let his heart die, then the primordial spirit wakes to life. To kill the heart does not mean to let it dry and wither away, but it means that it is undivided and gathered into one.

Buddha said: (When you fix your heart on one point, then nothing is impossible for you.) The heart easily runs away, so it is necessary to gather it together by means of breathing power. Breathing power easily becomes coarse, therefore it has to be refined by the heart. When that is done, can it then happen that it is not fixed?

The two mistakes of laziness and distraction must be combated by quiet work that is carried on daily without interruption; then results will certainly be achieved. If one is not seated during meditation, one will often be distracted without noticing it. To become conscious of the inattention is the mechanism by which to do away with inattention. Laziness of which a man is conscious, and laziness o f which he is unconscious, are many miles apart. Unconscious laziness is real laziness; conscious laziness is not complete laziness, because there is still some clarity in it. Distraction comes from letting the spirit wander about; laziness comes from the spirit not yet being pure. Distraction is much easier to correct than laziness. It is as in sickness if one feels pains and itches, one can help them with remedies, but laziness is like a disease that is attended by loss of feeling. Distraction can be overcome, confusion can be straightened out, but laziness and absent-minded are heavy and dark. Distraction and confusion at least have a place, but in laziness and absent-mindedness the anima alone is active. In inattention the animus is still present, but in laziness pure darkness rules. If one becomes sleepy during meditation, that is an effect of laziness. Breathing alone serves to remove laziness. Although the breath that flows in and out through the nose is not the true breath, the flowing in and out of the true breath is connected with it.

While sitting, one must, therefore, always keep the heart quiet and the power concentrated. How can the heart be made quiet? By breathing. The heart alone must be conscious of the flowing in and out of the breath; it must not be heard with the ears. If it is not heard, then the breathing is light; if light, it is pure. If it can be heard, then the breathing power is heavy; if heavy, then it is troubled; if it is troubled, then laziness and absent-mindedness develop and one wants to sleep. That is self-evident.

How to use heart correctly during breathing must be understood. It is use without use. One need only let the Light fall quite gently on the hearing. This sentence contains a secret meaning. What does it mean to let the Light fall? It is the radiance of the Light of one's own eyes. The eye looks inward and not outward. To sense brightness without looking outward means to look inward; it has nothing to do with an actual looking within. What does hearing mean? It is hearing the Light of one's own ear. The ear listens only within and does not listen to what is outside. To sense brightness without listening to what is outside, is to listen to what is within; it has nothing to do with actually listening to what is within. In this sort of hearing, one only hears that there is no sound; in this kind of seeing, one only sees that no shape is there. If the eye is not looking outward and the ear is not harkening outward, they close themselves and are inclined to sink inward. Only when one looks and harkens inward does the organ not go outward nor sink inward. In this way laziness and absent-mindedness are done away with. That is the union of the seed and the Light of the sun and moon.

If, as a result of laziness, one becomes sleepy, one should stand up and walk about. When the spirit has become clear one can sit down again. If there is time in the morning, one may sit during the burning of an incense candle, that is the best. In the afternoon, human affairs interfere and one can therefore easily fall into laziness. It is not necessary to have an incense candle. But one must lay aside all complications and sit quite still for a time. In the course of time there will be success without one's getting lazy and falling asleep.

MISTAKES DURING THE CIRCULATION OF THE LIGHT

Master Lu Tzu said: Your work will gradually draw itself together and mature, but before you reach the condition in which you sit like a withered tree before a cliff, there are many other possibilities of error which I would ;like to bring to your special attention. These conditions are only recognized when they have been personally experienced. I will enumerate them here, My school differs from the Buddhist yoga school, in that it has confirmatory signs for each step of the way. First I would like to speak of the mistakes and then the confirmatory signs.

When one sets out to carry out one's decision, care must be taken to see that everything can proceed in a comfortable, easy manner. Too much must not be demanded of the heart. On must be careful t hat, quite automatically, heart and power correspond to one another. Only then can a state of quietness be attained. During the quiet state the right conditions and the right place must be provided. One must not sit down (to meditate) in the midst of frivolous affairs. That is to say, one must not have any vacuities in the mind. All entanglements must be put aside and one must be supreme and independent. Nor must the thoughts be directed toward the right procedure. If too much trouble is taken there is danger of doing this. I do not mean that no trouble is to be taken, but the right behavior lies in the middle way between being and non-being. If one can attain purposelessness through purpose, then the thing has been grasped. Supreme and without confusion, one goes along in an independent way. Furthermore, one must not fall victim to the ensnaring world. The ensnaring world is where the five kinds of dark demons disport themselves.

This is the case, for example, when, after fixation, one has chiefly thoughts of dry wood and dead ashes, and few thoughts of the resplendent spring on the great earth. In this way one sinks into the world of darkness. The power is cold there, breathing is heavy, and many images of coldness and decay display themselves. If one tarries there long one enters the world of plants and stones.

Nor must a man be led astray by the ten thousand ensnarements. This happens if, after the quiet state has begun, one after another all sorts of ties suddenly appear. One wants to break through them and cannot; one follows them, and feels relieved by this. This means the matter has become a servant. If a man tarries in this state long he enters the world of illusory desires.

At best, one goes to Heaven; at the worst, one goes among the fox-spirits. Such a fox-spirit might also occupy himself in the famous mountains enjoying the wind and the moon, the flowers and fruits, and taking his pleasure in coral trees and jeweled grass. But after he has been occupied thus for three to five hundred years, or at the most, for a couple of thousand years, his reward is over and he is born again into the world of turmoil.

All of these are wrong paths. When a man knows the wrong paths, he can then inquire into the confirmatory signs.

CONFIRMATORY EXPERIENCES DURING THE CIRCULATION OF THE LIGHT

圖 胎 出

Master Lu Tzu said: There are many kinds of confirmatory experiences. One must not content oneself with small demands but must rise to the thought that all living creatures have to be freed. It is not permissible to be trivial and irresponsible in heart. One must strive to make deeds one's words.

If, when there is quiet, the spirit has continuously and uninterruptedly a sense of great gaiety as if intoxicated or freshly bathed, it is a sign that the Light principle in the whole body is harmonious; then the Golden Flower begins to bud. When, furthermore, all openings are quiet, and the silver moon stands in the middle of Heaven, and one has the feeling that the great earth is a world of light and brilliancy, that is a sign that the body of the heart opens itself to clarity. It is a sign that the Golden Flower is opening.

Furthermore, the whole body feels strong and firm so that it fears neither storm nor frost. Things by which other men are displeased, when I meet them, cannot cloud the brightness of the seed of the spirit. Yellow gold fills the house; the steps are white jade. Rotten and stinking things on earth that come in contact with one breath of true power will immediately live again. Red blood becomes milk. The fragile body of the flesh is sheer gold and diamonds. That is a sign that the Golden Flower is crystallized.

The Book of Successful contemplation says: The sun sinks in the Great Water and magic pictures of trees in rows arise. The setting sun means that in Chaos (in the world before phenomena, that is, intelligible world), a foundation is laid: that is the condition free of opposites. Highest good is like water, pure and spotless. It is the ruler of the Great Polarity, the god who is revealed in the sign for that which greatly disturbs, Chen. Chen is also symbolized by wood, wherefore the images of trees in rows appears. A sevenfold row of trees means the light of the seven body-openings (or heart-openings). In the northwest is the direction of the creative. When it moves on one place farther, the abysmal is there. The sun which sinking into the Great Water is the image for the creative and abysmal. The abysmal is the direction of midnight (mouse, north). At the winter solstice the thunder (Chen) is in the middle of the earth quite hidden and covered up. Only when the sign Chen is reached, does the Light-pole come over the earth again. That is the picture representing the row of trees. The rest can be correspondingly inferred.

The second part refers to the building of the foundation on this. The great world is like ice, a glassy world of jewels. The brilliancy of the Light is gradually crystallized. That is why a great terrace arises and upon it, in the course of time, Buddha appears. When the Golden Being appears who should it be but Buddha? For Buddha is the Golden Saint of the Great Enlightenment. This is a great confirmatory experience.

Now there are these confirmatory experiences which can be tested. The first is that, when one has entered the state of meditation, the gods are in the valley. Men are heard talking as though at a distance of several hundred paces, each one quite clear. But the sounds are all like an echo in a valley. One can always hear them, but never oneself. This is called the presence of the gods in the valley.

At times the following can be experienced: as soon as one is quiet, the Light of the eyes begins to blaze up, so that everything before one becomes quite bright as if one were in a cloud. If one opens one's eyes and seeks the body, it is not to be found any more. This is called: In the empty chamber it grows light. Inside and outside, everything is equally light. That is a very favorable sign. Or, when one sits in meditation, the fleshly body becomes quite shining like silk or jade. It seems difficult to remain sitting; one feels as if drawn upward. This is called: The spirit returns and pushes against Heaven. In time, one can experience it in such a way that one really floats upward.

And now it is possible to leave all three of these experiences. But not everything can be expressed. Different things appear to each person according to his gifts. If one experiences these things, it is a sign of a good aptitude. With these things it is just as it is when one drinks water. One can tell for oneself whether the water is swarm or cold. In the same way a man must convince himself about these experiences, then only are they real.

THE LIVING MANNER OF THE CIRCULATION OF THE LIGHT

Master Lu Tzu said: When there is gradual success in producing the circulation of the Light, a person must not give up their ordinary occupation in doing it. The ancients said: When occupations come to us, we must accept them; when things come to us, we must understand them from the ground up. If the occupations are regulated by correct thoughts, the Light is not scattered by outside things, but circulates according to its own law. Even the still-invisible circulation of the Light gets started this way, how much more then is it the case with the true circulation of the Light which has already manifested itself clearly. When in ordinary life one has the ability always to react to things by reflexes only, without any admixture of a thought of others or of himself, that is a circulation of the Light arising out of circumstances. It is the first secret.

A MAGIC SPELL FOR THE FAR JOURNEY

Master Lu Tzu said: Yu Ching has left behind him a magic spell
for the Far Journey:

Words crystallize the spirit in the place of power.
The sixth month the white snow is suddenly seen to fly.
The third watch the disk of the sun sends out shining rays.
The water blows the wind of gentleness.
Wandering in Heaven, one eats the spirit-power of the receptive.
The deeper secret within the secret:
land that is nowhere, that is the true home.

These verses are full of mystery. The meaning is: The most important thing in the Great Meaning is the four words: non-action in action. Non-action prevents a person from becoming entangled in form and image (substantiality). Action in non-action prevents a person from sinking into numbing emptiness and a dead nothingness. The effect is in the two eyes. The two eyes are like the pole of the Great Wain which turns the whole of creation; the cause the poles of Light and darkness to rotate. The Elixir depends from beginning to end on the One; the metal in the middle of the water, that is, the lead in the water-region. Heretofore we have spoken of the circulation of the Light, indicating thereby the initial release which works from without upon what lies within. This is to aid one in obtaining the Master. It is for the pupils in the beginning stages. They go through the two lower transitions in order to gain the upper one. After the sequence of events is clear and the nature of the release is known, Heaven no longer withholds the Meaning, but reveals the ultimate truth. Disciples keep it secret and hold to it strictly!

The circulation of the Light is the inclusive term. The further the work advances, the more can the Golden Flower bloom. But there is a still more marvelous kind of circulation. Til now we have worked from the outside on what is within; now we tarry in the center and rule what is external. Hitherto, it was a service in aid of the Master; now it is a dissemination of the commands of this Master. The whole relationship is now reversed. If one wants to penetrate the more delicate regions by this method, one must first see to it that the body and heart are completely controlled, that one is quite free and at peace, letting go of all entanglements, untroubled by the slightest excitement, with the Heavenly Heart exactly in the middle. Then let one lower the lids of the two eyes as if one received a holy edict, a summons to the minister. Who would dare disobey? Then one illumines the house of the abysmal (water) with both eyes. Wherever the Golden Flower appears, the true Light of polarity goes out to meet it. The principle of that which adheres to (lightness), is light outside and dark within; it is the body of the creative. Darkness enters and becomes master. The results is that the heart (consciousness), becomes dependent on things, is directed outward, and is tossed about on the stream. When the rotating Light shines within the heart, it does not become dependent on things, the power of the dark is limited, and the Golden Flower shines with concentration. It is then the collected Light of polarity. Things that are related attract each other. Thus does the polarity Light-line of the abysmal press upward. It is not only the Light in the abyss, but it is creative Light meeting creative Light. As soon as these two substances meet each other, they unite inseparably, and unceasing life begins; it comes and goes, and rises and falls of itself, in the house of primordial power. One is aware of effulgence and infinity. The whole body feels lighter and would like to fly. This is the state of which it is said: Clouds fill the thousand mountains. Gradually it (life) goes here and there quite quietly; it rises and falls imperceptibly. The pulse stands still and breathing stops. This is the moment of true creative unity, the state of which it is said: The moon gathers up the ten thousand waters. In the midst of this darkness, the Heavenly Heart suddenly begins a movement. This is the return of the one Light, the time when the child comes to life.

But the details of this must be carefully explained. When a person looks at something, listens to something, eyes and ears move and follow the things until they have passed. These movements are all underlings, and when the Heavenly ruler follows them in their tasks, it means: To live together with demons.

If now, during every movement and every moment of rest, a person lives together with people and not with demons, then the Heavenly ruler is the t rue man. When he moves and we move with him, the movement is the root of Heaven. When he is quiet and we are quiet with him, this quietness is the cave of the moon. When he continues to alternate movement and quietness, one ought to go on with him unceasingly in movement and quietness. If he rises and falls with inhaling and exhaling, we must rise and fall with him. That is what is called going to and fro between the root of Heaven and the cave of the moon.

When the Heavenly Heart still preserves calm, movement before the right time is a fault of softness. When the Heavenly Heart has already moved, the movement that follows afterwards, corresponding with it, is a fault or rigidity. As soon as the Heavenly Heart is stirring, one must immediately mount with all one's feeling to the house of the creative. Thus the Light of the spirit sees the summit that is the leader. This movement is in accord with the time. The Heavenly Heart rises to the summit of the creative, where it expands in complete freedom. Then suddenly it wants the deepest silence, and one must lead it speedily and with one's whole being into the yellow castle. Thus the eyes behold the central yellow dwelling place of the spirit.

When the desire for silence comes, not a single thought arises; he who is looking inward suddenly forgets that he looks. At this time, body and heart must be left completely free. All entanglements disappear without trace. Then I no longer know at what place the house of my spirit and my crucible are. If a man wants to make certain of his body, he cannot get at it. This condition is the penetration of Heaven into earth, the time when all wonders return to their roots.

The One is the circulation of the Light. If one begins, it is at first scattered and one tries to collect it; the six senses are not active. This is the care and nourishment of one's own origin, the filling up of the oil when one goes to receive life. When one is far enough to have gathered it, one feels light and free and need take no further trouble. This is the quieting of the spirit in the space of the ancestors, the taking possession of former Heaven.

When one is so far advanced that every shadow and every echo has disappeared, so that one is quiet and firm, it is safe within the cave of power, where all that is miraculous returns to its roots. The place is not changed but divides itself. It is incorporeal space where a thousand and ten thousand places are one place. The time is not changed, but divides itself. It is immeasurable time when all the eons are like a moment.

As long as the heart has not attained complete peace, it cannot move itself. One moves the movement and forgets the movement; this is not movement in itself. Therefore it is said: If, when stimulated by external things, one is moved, it is the instinct of the being. If, when not stimulated by external things, one is moved, it is the movement of Heaven. The being that is placed over against Heaven, can fall and come under the domination of the instincts. The instincts are based upon the fact that there are external things. They are thoughts that go on beyond their own position. Then movement leads to movement. But, when no idea arises, the right ideas come. That is the true idea. If things are quiet and one is quite firm, the release of

Heaven suddenly moves. Is this not a movement without purpose? Action in inaction has the same meaning.

As to the beginning of the poem, the first two lines refer entirely to the activity of the Golden Flower. The two next lines are concerned with the mutual interpenetration of sun and moon. The sixth month is the adhering fire. The white snow that flies, is the true darkness of polarity in the middle of the fire sign, that is about to turn into the receptive. The third watch is the abysmal water. The sun's disk is the one polar line in the sign for water, which is about to turn into the creative. In this is contained the way to take the sign for the abysmal and the way to reverse the sign for the adhering fire. The following two lines have to do with the activity of the pole of the Great Wain, the rise and fall of the whole release of polarity. Water is the sign of the abysmal; the eye is the wind of softness. The light of the eyes illumines the house of the abysmal, and controls there the seed of the great Light. "In Heaven" means the house of the creative. "Wandering, in Heaven, one eats the spirit-power of the receptive." This shows how the spirit penetrates the power, and how Heaven penetrates the earth; this happens so that the fire can be nourished.

Other books from

Freemasonry

Look to the East
- Ralph P. Lester
Morals and Dogma
- Albert Pike
Duncan's Ritual and Monitor of Freemasonry
- Malcolm C. Duncan
Ritual of the Order of the Eastern Star
- F. A. Bell
Meaning of Masonry
- W.L Wilmshurst
Exposition of Freemasonry – Illustrated
- WM. Morgan

Philosophy

Politics
- Aristotle
Republic
- Plato
The Advancement of Learning
- Francis Bacon
The Interpretation of Dreams
-   Sigmund Freud
HAGAKURE - Selections (The Way of the Samurai)
- Yamamoto Tsunetomo